Acts of
Recovery

The Story of One Man's Ongoing Healing
from Sexual Abuse by a Priest

MICHAEL D. HOFFMAN

acta
PUBLICATIONS

ACTS OF RECOVERY
The Story of One Man's Ongoing Healing
from Sexual Abuse by a Priest
by Michael D. Hoffman

Edited by Gregory F. Augustine Pierce
Cover design, interior design, and typesetting by Patricia A. Lynch

Copyright © 2013 by Michael D. Hoffman

Published by ACTA Publications, 4848 N. Clark Street, Chicago, IL 60640,
(800) 397-2282, www.actapublications.com

All rights reserved. No part of this publication may be reproduced or
transmitted in any form or by any means, electronic, digital, or mechanical,
including photocopying and recording, or by any information storage
and retrieval system, including the Internet, without permission from the
publisher. Permission is hereby given to use short excerpts with proper
citation in reviews and marketing copy, newsletters, bulletins, class handouts,
and scholarly papers.

ISBN: 978-0-87946-517-9
Printed in the United States of America by Total Printing Systems
Year 20 19 18 17 16 15 14 13
Printing 12 11 10 9 8 7 6 5 4 3 2 First

♻ Text printed on 30% post-consumer recycled paper.

Contents

Dedication

To my parents Darryl and Mary Ellen Hoffman — I didn't want to tell you. Even as an adult, I didn't want to tell you. Now having told you, I hope and pray we can recover the good times and restore the sacred family bonds we almost lost because of this abuse.

To my sister Julie and brother Tom — the devastating reality of the abuse and the effects my abuser had on our family profoundly changed us and our relationships with one another. It is sad and painful, but true. I hope there can be peace in your hearts as all of us raise our own children and do whatever we can to protect them from the heartache we experienced.

To my wife Kathy — telling you my story of abuse was the single most important act of recovery for me. I didn't want to hold back such a huge part of my life from you, but I was afraid. You listened to me, heard the depth of my sorrow, and still loved me. That's all I ever wanted.

To our children Colleen and Michael — if something bad happens to you, please don't hold onto it for 30 years like I did. If you can talk about it, even if you don't know exactly what to say, you will live a fuller, more complete, and happier life.

Introduction

This book is not intended to be an exposé of what the Catholic Church, or specifically in my case the Archdiocese of Chicago, did or did not do regarding the sexual abuse of me and other children by certain priests, deacons, or religious. Much has been, and will continue to be, written on that subject.

Instead, this book is the story of my journey to recover from the effects of childhood sexual abuse imposed upon me by a Catholic priest starting when I was 12 years old. My efforts to find healing and hope from underneath terrible sadness and pain involves many people and is intertwined with the same Church that allowed my abuser to remain in ministry at the time.

The man who sexually abused me, it turned out, abused many other children as well. He was moved from parish to parish by archdiocesan officials. In fact, he was placed in eight parishes throughout the Archdiocese of Chicago. One day in 1993, a courageous family sued him in court and won. He was convicted of sexual abuse of a minor and was sentenced to three years in prison. He resigned his priesthood in 1994, and the Vatican finally vacated his priesthood in 2010. His name and photo are now on the Archdiocese of Chicago website list of abusive priests. The Vicar for Priests for the archdiocese at the time was deposed in 2007 as part of an ongoing mediation process with clergy abuse victims. His deposition is also posted on the Archdiocese of Chicago website.

It is extremely difficult for me to write about my abuser and those who enabled him. Those years of my life, aged 12-16, any child's most formative years, are like a low, grey cloud of emotional stress and upheaval. My abuser was a close friend of my parents. They felt that any time I spent with him would be a quality experience, a mentoring relationship. He was charismatic and funny, an excellent public speaker who wrote and delivered challenging homilies. In fact, just to let you know the deepness of the relationship with my parents and give you a glimpse at his profound betrayal of their friendship, they once gave him a local artist's hand-crafted ceramic chalice and paten, which was used by him at Mass. My parents took great pride that he used their gift so often. This should give you a sense of the deeply rooted Catholic identity my parents instilled in me and the complete and total devastation they felt when they finally realized this priest friend had sexually abused their son.

I am not going to write about that sick man and his enablers in this book. I am not going to give details of the abuse. That is my choice, and I hope you will respect it.

As an adult survivor of childhood sexual abuse, a practicing Catholic, and a husband and father of two children, I am trying now to understand and reconcile in my life the trauma I experienced at the hands of my abuser and how those painful memories affect me today. My healing journey includes my family, my friends, other survivors of childhood abuse, and certain priests and staff of the Archdiocese of Chicago, including Francis Cardinal George, OMI.

For over 30 years, I didn't tell anybody my story of abuse. I held back these traumatic moments in my life because I was ashamed of what happened to me and afraid of what other people were going to think. Once I decided to tell my story, I realized I didn't have to hold back anymore. I could be myself.

I have written these pages for my own therapeutic benefit, but also to offer my name and face and voice to help heal the heartache and pain other child sexual abuse survivors and their families face each and every day. I hope to provide leadership and vision on this difficult issue, especially as it has affected my Church and society. As a committed Catholic, I firmly believe in God's grace and the power of reconciliation. If these goals and guidelines are acceptable to you, then I invite you to read the story of my ongoing recovery.

Prologue

One of my most vivid memories is of the time Dad and I went to see the first *Star Wars* movie, over 30 years ago. I remember just the two of us spending most of the day together. It was opening day for this movie, and we went to an afternoon show. We had been curious about this movie for so long. It was billed as a real action-packed sci-fi adventure film, a film like no other. Dad was excited to see it, and I was excited to spend time with him.

We left early for the theater because we expected there would be a line, and there was. When we got there, Dad dropped me off so I could run and get in line while he parked the car. We got to talking with some of the people who were excited to see the movie too. The wait didn't seem too bad to me, and before long we had purchased the tickets and were finding our seats.

Dad was always great to go to the movies with. He had no problem buying the large popcorn, candy, and a large drink. For a boy, that makes your day. I was totally happy. We sat in our seats eating the popcorn and candy together, waiting for the movie to begin. I remember feeling life was good.

After the previews, there was a long pause. Then the great *Star Wars* theme music thundered over the theater and the chapter story, "A New Hope" scrolled along the screen. Then immediately we were shown the underbelly of the largest space ship we had ever seen, the Imperial Star Destroyer. My eyes flew open wide, and I looked up at Dad, and he looked down at me, and we both smiled. We knew this was going to be great.

And it was.

It is a great memory for me, and this memory has become even more important to me recently. Seeing *Star Wars* with Dad and spending the whole afternoon together was such a good and decent time. It is one of my last memories of me just being a kid and having fun. That day was pure joy and innocence to me, the way it is supposed to be for a young boy.

I do have many other memories of my teen years, but they are clouded memories, discolored by a man, our parish priest at the time, who did terrible things to me. This man sexually abused me for close to four years, starting very soon after that perfect day with my father.

I was 12 years old.

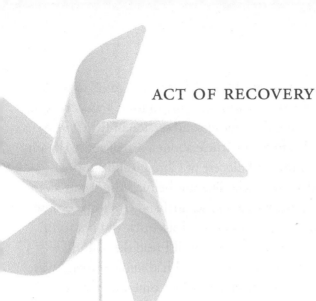

ACT OF RECOVERY

Kathy

My wife Kathy and I live in the far northwest corner of the city of Chicago. It is a great neighborhood. Most of the homes are brick and were built in the early 1940s. We have two kids, Colleen (age 16) and Michael (age 14). Kathy and I have been married 19 years. In July, 2006, I told her my story of being sexually abused by a priest. Telling Kathy what happened to me as a boy has been and remains my primary act of recovery.

My morning work routine involves a 5:30 am wake up. I go downstairs to our kitchen and drink a couple of cups of coffee and read the newspaper. The house is quiet and peaceful then, and I use this time to relax, reflect, and breathe. After about 20 minutes, I eat breakfast, shower, then go off to work.

On June 14, 2006, it was the same routine. I was drinking my coffee and reading the Chicagoland section of the *Chicago Tribune*. I stumbled upon an article about a sexual abuse lawsuit being filed against the Archdiocese of Chicago and a former priest. I had read a few articles like this before. Also, I was aware of the recent Boston sexual abuse scandal and cover-up because it received national media attention. This article did not seem to be different from all the others, until I read the plaintiff's names. There were names of two boys I had known when I was younger. At various times, they were in the room with me and this man. There were often a lot of boys in the room.

I had to keep it together.

I read the article once, and then I read it again. I stood up: my heart was pounding. I walked around the kitchen and read the article a third time. The names of the boys I knew, along with the name of my abuser and the places of abuse set off in me anxiety, heart palpitations, and sweating. However, I was self-employed and had to go to work, so I had a bowl of cereal, showered, got dressed, and left. It was my routine. I had an appointment. I had to keep it together.

But on that day I began to realize that the sexual activity I had endured as a child was perverse and depraved, wrong and criminal. This man had been a friend of our family, and he framed our physical encounters as normal affection or ways in which normal people show love. I began that day to understand what he had imposed upon me was not normal and not love but was in fact traumatic and very painful abuse.

On that day, while I wept and shook with complete exhaustion, struggling with the memories, I began to heal from the repressed and long-lasting effects of childhood sexual abuse. I call what happened "acts of recovery," and I hope to tell about them here.

I left the house that morning. Kathy and the kids were still sleeping. As I got into my car I thought "what is going on with me?" I pulled away from the curb and started crying. I was shaking. I had vivid memories of the taste of his cigar in my mouth. You see, the primary way this man greeted me in his room at the rectory was with an open-mouthed kiss. He did it to all the boys, and he did it to me too. Tears were streaming down my face as I drove that morning. I remembered alcohol, marijuana, and adult pornography on the television. I remembered many boys in the room, some older, some younger than me. I remembered group masturbation, backrubs, oral sex acts. It all came back to me.

I continued driving. The tears were now slow and steady. I was so sad. I realized that these memories, even though I had repressed them, upset me and undermined my attempts at being happy in life. I suddenly felt a mammoth weight pressing on me — anxiety, emotional and physical exhaustion, depression about my life and being a victim of childhood abuse, and fear about what to do next. This burden was totally consuming, yet I did not know what to do with it. I kept driving to my first appointment of the day, wiped the tears from my face, and went in to see my customer. I was happy to have something else to think about, even though I knew it would only be a short relief from these terrible thoughts and memories. I had no co-workers I could confide in or ask for help. There was no one to call to cover me if I decided to take a sick day. I felt isolated and alone.

Throughout the remainder of that day and the next, I struggled with the recollections of the perverse and depraved behavior of my abuser and what he had done to me. I did not sleep or eat well. I was a man going through the motions at work and at home. I was emotionally distracted from Kathy and the kids, distant and unavailable, lost in my thoughts about the trauma I had endured. The following day was Saturday.

I was a man going through the motions at work and at home.

Like most families with kids, it was very busy at our house on the weekends. It was mid-June. Michael played baseball and Colleen played softball with our local park district league. Both Kathy and I were coaches. Even with a lack of sleep and the constant anxiety from the past two days, this Saturday morning, on the surface, looked like any typical Saturday.

The kids were in their uniforms. We were checking their bat bags to make sure they had everything. We filled coolers with water to take to the game. Kathy and Colleen went off to their game, Michael and I to ours. I was upset with myself because what should have been a pleasant time with my son felt intolerable. I thought I might be unable to make it through the game. I become completely distracted and didn't think I could take it anymore. I could no longer pretend that nothing happened. I had to tell Kathy. But how?

We got through the game. I cannot recall if we won or lost. After the game, Michael asked a friend to come over to our house for lunch. We returned home, and soon after Kathy and Colleen arrived. Colleen had also asked one of her girlfriends to come over. Kathy changed out of her coach's shirt and had to go grocery shopping and run some errands. I was home with the kids and their friends, almost paralyzed with anxiety and fear about telling my wife the story of my childhood abuse.

Kathy and I have a wonderful family together. We have beautiful, healthy kids. We have been blessed in so many ways. I felt that we were all in a good place — happy, safe, and secure. I was fearful to introduce into our relationship such an odd, sick story. I didn't think Kathy could possibly understand. In fact, I didn't really understand at the time all that had happened to me and how the abuse had affected me. I had irrational thoughts: Kathy would think differently of me; I would no longer be the man she married; she would think, "How could a victim of abuse ever get over it, ever be a good provider?" I didn't know what I was going to say to her, but I realized I had to tell her and felt it had to be today. Otherwise, I was certain I would have a nervous breakdown. And so, on this typically busy Saturday, with the kids having friends over and Kathy in and out of the house running errands, I did it. I pulled her aside and told her I had to talk with her. I asked her to come upstairs so the kids couldn't hear. I took her into Michael's room and closed the door. I have never seen her so concerned. What could possibly be so urgent and important?

She sat down. My hands were shaking. My voice cracked and my heart raced. She told me I was making her nervous. I said I had something terrible to tell her, and with tears in my eyes I told my wife of over a decade that when I was a boy, I had been sexually abused for years by a local parish priest.

She listened to me and believed me immediately.

Kathy and I were in Michael's room for about 10 minutes. It is 10 minutes I will never forget. I shared with her one of the most intensely personal stories anyone can share with another human being. The depth of sadness and pain that came out of me shocked her, but she listened to me intently and believed me immediately. I cannot remember exactly what she said to me at the time. As I think back on it, it didn't really matter what she said. The act of telling her my story and having her listen to me changed my life in ways that I am still coming to appreciate. Telling her that I had been repeatedly sexually abused was one of the most difficult things I ever had to do, but I am so glad I did it. Eventually, I wiped the tears from my face, Kathy told me how much she loved me, and we went back downstairs.

The kids were still playing in the basement with their friends. They were unaware anything had happened. I had been consumed with anxiety and fear, and now that I had told Kathy I had many questions about what was going to happen. What do I do now? How do people in our situation move forward? How could I ever get over the anxiety and terrible sadness I had been feeling for the past three days? I must admit that it was good to have a busy household that weekend. The kids still needed attention, and Kathy and I had previously planned to go out to dinner that night. These "normal" aspects of our family life took on new meaning for both of us right away. I guess I thought that once I told Kathy, I could return to my normal self. For a few hours afterward I felt much better. I was relieved. I was optimistic.

But the healing had only just begun.

ACT OF RECOVERY

Fr. Greg

Kathy and I agreed to never tell our family or friends about what had happened to me. I felt like a rape victim, which I was, but in a different way. It had happened so long ago. I had been so young at the time. My memories of the events have been filtered through the lens of a terrified 12-year-old boy. I felt that if I came forward to tell my story now, people would question the character of the victim, not the predator — just as they do to so many victims of rape and other heinous crimes. Kathy and I didn't want that. So we decided to keep the entire thing quiet. In fact, Kathy and I did not talk about it too much with one another. It was almost like, "Well, that's that. I told her and now we can get on with our lives."

I continued thinking about it a lot, however. I was wondering, "Is telling Kathy enough? Is that all I need to do?" I was happy I had told her, but I wondered if there was more I needed.

I have observed that it is difficult for some men to make and keep good friends. I am one of them. I have always wanted to have good friends, but I have always held back. Now I know why. Even subconsciously, I felt that if others knew I was sexually abused as a child, especially by a priest,

"Is telling Kathy all I need to do?"

they would think I was odd and not want to be around me. I think staying aloof was a way for me to hide my shame by concealing the painful stories of my childhood — stories I had buried so deep I didn't even know they were there myself. Up until recently, these inhibitions greatly restricted my social life and my ability to make and keep good friends.

Kathy and I are over at Mick and Karen O'Rourke's home quite often. Mick and Karen are very special friends to us. We can be at their home for a Saturday afternoon beer after one of our children's baseball games, or we can sit down for dinner with them or one or two other couples. Many times, we are invited to participate in their family parties. Through this friendship, I have realized the power of telling stories. When friends get together and feel comfortable, they tell stories about themselves as a way to let people know who they are. The O'Rourke's make friends by telling stories about themselves and listening to others as they tell stories about themselves.

But in these social settings, when friends were telling stories about their childhoods, if it was my turn I would always change the subject or make a funny comment about something else. I didn't even realize I was doing this. I was holding back, always with my guard up, not letting people get to know me. After my conversation with Kathy, I realized I had to make a change. I was inspired by the simple idea of Mick and Karen telling sad, sweet, funny stories about themselves and in so doing allowing people into their lives and letting people know who they are. I wanted to be like them. I had some more work to do before I could do that, however.

We are active parishioners at St. Mary of the Woods Catholic Church on the northwest side of the City of Chicago. We live about one block from the church and the Catholic school where our children attend. It is a vibrant parish where so many people who care about their Catholic faith volunteer at the parish and the school. It is a close-knit faith community with the long-standing tradition of coming together to help people in need. Most recently, two of our friends had been diagnosed with breast cancer, and a group of women asked for volunteers to cook dinners for these families as they began their chemotherapy and radiation treatments. Thirty different people volunteered immediately. There are many other similar stories over the years of this parish coming out in support of those who have suffered the death of a sick child, loss of a spouse, serious illness, financial difficulties, and many other traumas and crises we all must endure from time to time. We have made great friends at St. Mary of the Woods, and Kathy and I are very comfortable there. We also feel it is a great example for our children to see so many adults volunteering for the betterment of the church, school, and community.

I am inspired by the priests at our parish. We have had and continue to have a long line of good men as pastors, associates, and visitors. I believe in them and the ministry they and the other staff members do, and I believe in the parish community. Kathy and I are regular church-goers. We do not have a perfect record by any means, but it is important to us that we attend church regularly. As I came to terms with my sexual abuse, I began to feel strongly that I should tell one of our priests, our pastor at the time, Fr. Greg Sakowicz.

I had to think about this for a few days. I really wanted to tell him. I wanted to continue to feel comfortable going to church at SMOW (as it is affectionately called). I was also becoming very anxious at the idea of telling him, in part because I had never told anyone except Kathy and also because I worried about what Fr. Greg would think. It would be my first time verbalizing my story in detail to anyone in the outside world. Could I handle it? Could he? Would he believe that one of his fellow priests had done such things to me? Over the next several days, I suppressed this idea of telling Fr. Greg, but it just kept coming back to me. It realized that I did have a need to talk with someone other than Kathy. I was still struggling with recovered memories of the abuse, and I was exhausted from the personal struggle. I felt very isolated not being able to talk freely to someone other than my wife about one of the most tragic events in my life. Even for Kathy, the subject of my sexual abuse was too shocking and too distracting from everyday life to discuss on a regular basis.

One day, while I was driving around for work, I just did it. I picked up the cell phone and called the rectory at SMOW. I asked to speak with Fr. Greg. My heart was pounding in my chest. The receptionist sent me to his voicemail. I left a short message telling him I needed to make an appointment. I hung up. My heart rate was still high. I was nervous to trust any priest with this deeply personal and sad story. I realized I was still terrified of telling anyone.

I kept all of my appointments throughout that day. On the outside, I maintained a professional appearance and conducted business as usual, but on the inside I was really struggling. I had a constant churning in my stomach. I was perspiring all the time, and I became self-conscious about that.

Near the end of the workday, Fr. Greg called me back on my cell phone. My heart instantly started racing again. I am usually very talkative with Fr. Greg. He loves to tell jokes, and usually we exchange one or two, but on this phone call I just blurted out that I needed to make an appointment to see him as soon as possible. He didn't ask me why — thank God! We picked a date and time. He then proceeded to tell me a typical corny Fr. Greg joke, which I was thankful for because it did make me smile, and we hung up. My heart rate began to slow. As I continued driving home I thought, "Can I handle any more stress?"

A few days later, I rang the doorbell to the rectory. I had been in this building many times, but this time was different. My heart was racing again, and I had a constant churning in my stomach. The receptionist opened the door, and I smiled weakly and said I had an appointment with Fr. Greg. I entered the building completely aware of how utterly tired I was.

After a few moments, Fr. Greg came around the corner. He was carrying some paperwork, so he suggested I go into his office while he put away his papers. His office was full of personal photos, sports memorabilia, and books of all kinds. This calmed me down. I continued to gaze at some of the photos as Fr. Greg walked in and closed the door. We made the usual pleasantries. I knew I was stalling, but I just didn't know how to begin.

"Mike, why are you here?"

Finally, Fr. Greg interrupted me. "Mike, why are you here?" I stared blankly back at him for a moment, my heart racing faster than ever before. I took a deep breath and began my next act of recovery: I told my priest my story of being sexually abused by another priest as a child. Fr. Greg's eyes opened wide as we talked. He didn't know what to say, but he listened carefully, and then we talked for close to an hour.

I walked out of the rectory in total disbelief. I never thought I could tell anyone other than my wife, much less a priest, what had happened to me. But I did it, and the world did not crash down around me. I experienced a feeling of indescribable relief. As hard as it was, I was happy I had told Fr. Greg what had happened to me.

I didn't realize it at the time, but this was the second act of my recovery.

ACT OF RECOVERY

Sam Bell

After telling Kathy and Fr. Greg about the abuse I had suffered as a child, I lived with it for a while. I tried to understand how I felt having told two people my story. I had no other comparative experience to draw on. I was in unchartered waters and at this point was unsettled in many areas. I am so thankful to Kathy for keeping such a normal household at this time. Our focus never wavered from our kids, school activities, sporting events, friends, and family. Fr. Greg kept in touch, asking how things were going, offering to help, but allowing me to make the next move.

My recollections of abuse, which had come rushing back

once they had finally emerged, had taken over my entire focus, all of my energy. The memories upset me greatly. I was so sad that I cried almost daily. I had near constant anxiety and was at least mildly depressed. I was emotionally distracted from my wife and kids. I began to feel that I should tell my story to someone within the Archdiocese of Chicago. I tried to imagine how I should go about doing this and what it might be like. Would reporting the abuse to Church officials be helpful and healing to me and others, or would it only add to my stress? My biggest fear was that they would not believe me.

At the time, there was a general-practice attorney in the office building of my company named Sam Bell. I used to run into Sam in the hallway several times each week. We had been in the same office building for several years and over time had gotten to know one another. I liked Sam. He met my kids when I took them to the office, and he has two grown children. I began thinking that I should talk with Sam about my situation.

I am not used to talking with attorneys. My only experience with lawyers had been for our real estate closings and to prepare our will. Other than that, I had never needed legal advice. It felt very strange to be thinking about talking with an attorney about something so personal and embarrassing. I did not know what to expect from Sam, but the more I thought about it the more I wanted to file a claim with the Archdiocese of Chicago. I did not want it to get out of hand, however. I didn't want my name in the papers or a civil suit filed or any kind of publicity like that. I needed an attorney I could talk to and trust and who would listen to me.

For some reason, I knew Sam was the guy. I struggled with how to get the conversation started. From casual conversation with someone in the hallway at work to describing in detail horrific stories of abuse done to me by a Catholic priest when I was a child seemed an impossibly great leap. I was uncertain how to broach the subject, afraid of losing what little control I still had over my emotions. But the idea of telling Sam kept coming back to me, and Kathy and I talked about whether or not it would be a good idea.

One afternoon I just did it.

One afternoon I just did it. I passed Sam's office and saw he was not busy. I knocked on his door, and he invited me in. With my heart racing, I asked Sam if he had a few minutes to talk with me. My tone was very serious — far different from our usual casual conversation. Sam sensed this and asked me to sit down. After a short, awkward pause, I took a deep breath and told him my story. I did virtually all the talking. Sam sat there with his mouth open. I'll bet he never expected to have a client like me walk into his office!

I told Sam everything, even details I had yet to share with Kathy or Fr. Greg. I finished by telling him that I was an active Catholic in our parish and did not want any publicity. (I still felt, as has happened many times during the sexual abuse scandals in the Church, that the moral character of the victims was often questioned more than that of the perpetrators.) Then

I asked for his help in approaching the archdiocese. He had a few questions, and at the end of our conversation he suggested we write a letter to officials of the Archdiocese of Chicago and see how they responded. I thought this was the right next step and retained his services on the spot.

I left Sam's office a bit shaken but relieved that it had gone so well. A few days later, Sam asked me to approve a copy of the letter he wanted to send before it went out. I am glad he asked, because I wanted to stay in control of the entire process. The letter looked good to me: factual, non-threatening, respectful yet firm. Mailing this letter began a long chain of difficult and painful events that would profoundly affect my wife and kids, my sister and brother, and finally my parents. It would change my life dramatically for the better. It was sent only six weeks after my first reading of the June 14 *Chicago Tribune* article.

Meeting with Sam and sending the letter was my third act of recovery.

Dr. Bland and Leah McCluskey

Sam's letter went out in the mail. I had shown a copy to Kathy before it did. We were both still a bit nervous about the story getting out and what people might say. We wanted to protect our children from any ignorant or insensitive comments people might make. We also had a vague sense that something larger was about to happen, and we could not predict what the outcome would be. That was unsettling to us both, but we decided to proceed.

I continued on with work. Throughout each day I thought about my abuser and the acts of abuse he forced upon me. I was pre-occupied with numerous questions about the past. How could I have let this happen? Why didn't I tell my parents? Why didn't anybody ask any questions about what that priest was doing with all the young boys up in his room in the rectory? Why didn't my parents, or any other parents of the other boys who were also abused, realize that their sons were in anguish? How could the Church let this priest go on abusing children for so long? I had no answers to any of these questions, but I kept concluding that my life was a mess. I suffered terrible sadness and heartache and uncertainty as to how any of this could possibly resolve itself.

About a week after the letter went out, Sam Bell received a call from the Archdiocese of Chicago from a woman named Leah McCluskey, the Professional Responsibility Administrator. Sam called me that afternoon and asked me to come to his office, which I did, full of trepidation as I walked in. We made small talk to start, but I was eager for him to get to the subject. It is always difficult to transition from normal, regular, polite conversation to the difficult subject of childhood sexual abuse.

Sam finally said a representative of the archdiocese had called and wanted to meet me. I was slow to comprehend this. We had written one short letter and they wanted to meet me? I remember there was a long pause, an uncomfortable silence in the room. My heart had started to pound and my mind was racing. I didn't know what I expected, but it was not this. I finally asked Sam, "What do they want to talk about?" Sam told me that apparently there is a process in place where any person abused by a priest can tell his or her story to someone in the archdiocese, and that information is then presented to a Review

Board to determine if there is reasonable cause to suspect the priest of sexual misconduct.

It was difficult for me to process this information, but finally I was relieved to learn there is already a system in place where I could tell my story. I immediately questioned, however, whether I would have the courage to do this after 30 years of suppressed memories. I could only imagine the difficulty I would have sitting before any Church official telling my story. This idea would have been unthinkable to me when the abuse was happening — the idea of a young 12-year-old boy telling a Church official that a priest had repeatedly done unthinkable things to me. But I am a grown man now. With my heart literally pounding through my chest, I told Sam I would do it and asked him to make the call to set up the meeting.

Were they going to believe this incredible story?

I left Sam's office and went back to my own. I was totally exhausted, slumped down in my chair, totally useless for work. I sat and stared at the wall. The phone rang several times, but I did not pick it up. The fax machine was printing out orders, but I did not look at them. I was completely incapable of dealing with anything else right then. The burden was too great. I couldn't imagine what would happen next. Would the archdiocesan officials believe me? What if they didn't? I was only 12 years old when the abuse happened. Were they going to believe this incredible story 30 years later? Wouldn't it be better to simply let it go and not say anything to anyone, to just try and forget the abuse ever happened?

I finally left the office and went home to talk it over with Kathy. It was August, however, and I met her and the kids at a local swimming pool. I thanked God for this. This was normal family fun and I needed some relief. Some of our friends and their families were at the pool as well, and I was able to relax a little bit. I held off telling Kathy until we got home that night and the kids were in bed. We discussed what I should do, but we didn't make a final decision on whether or not to proceed.

I had a regular workday scheduled the next day. After my first appointment, I received a call on my cell from Sam. He told me he called the archdiocese back and they gave him a couple of dates within the next two weeks to consider. My head was spinning. It seemed everything was going too fast. But I picked a date, August 24, 2006. I hung up, stopped driving, and began to cry. Why me? Why did it have to be me?

I wiped the tears from my face and started driving again. I kept the remainder of my appointments that day, comforted by the regular routine of my job. When I got home I told Kathy I was anxious about meeting with the archdiocese but that it seemed to me to be the right thing to do. She supported me. She always does.

I went over the story in my head, over and over, day after day. I had to meet my responsibilities with my company, but I kept thinking of the various acts of abuse by this priest that I had endured as a child. I didn't eat or sleep well during this time.

On the morning of August 24, just 10 weeks after reading the *Chicago Tribune* article, I dressed in a business suit and tie. There was not much to say to Kathy. She and the kids had summertime activities planned for the day. She gave me a hug and left with them. I sat and waited for Sam to pick me up. We made pleasant conversation on the way into the city, which was a nice distraction for me. But my heart began to race as we got closer to the archdiocesan headquarters. We found parking, walked across the street, and went into the office building.

Quickly we were greeted and escorted into a conference room. Sam and I were briefly alone. We had nothing left to say to each other. I did not want to sit down. I was that nervous. After a few moments, there was a knock on the door. Dr. Michael Bland entered and introduced himself. He said he was a consultant with the Archdiocese of Chicago working with the Archdiocese Office of Assistance Ministry on sexual abuse cases. He seemed like a nice enough guy. He asked me to sit down and began to give us an overview of what would happen at the meeting that day. He gave us basic information about the Review Board process, then asked me to introduce myself. I told him, "I am Michael Hoffman, and I was sexually abused as a child by a priest who was then associate pastor at St. Mary's parish in Lake Forest." There. I had said to someone in authority what I had been afraid to say for 30 years.

Dr. Bland thanked me for coming and told us that another person would run the interview and take notes. He left the room to get her. A moment later, they both returned. Leah

McCluskey, the Professional Responsibility Administrator for the Archdiocese of Chicago, introduced herself. She seemed very nice, and I immediately felt comfortable with her. Sam was just an observer now. We all sat down. Ms. McCluskey mentioned a few more details related to how the meeting would go and then asked if I wished to tell my story. My heart was pounding yet again, and I had the feeling I was sweating through my shirt. It had taken me 30 years to get to this moment, and now here it was. All eyes were on me now. It was an indescribable feeling, akin to how it must feel to jump off a cliff into unknown waters. When I was 12, I felt I could never tell my parents that this priest "friend" of our family had repeatedly done horrible things to me. I didn't think they would believe me. Thirty years later, I wondered if the two nice people in that room would believe me now.

It had taken me 30 years to get to this moment, and now here it was.

I took a deep breath and began to tell my story. I lost my composure early on, due to the sheer magnitude of the moment, but I calmed down and continued. That testimony was by far the most difficult thing I have ever had to do. All of the confusing, disturbing, and sick feelings I had about my relationship with my abuser finally tumbled out of me. I gave details I had never told anyone, including Kathy. It was exhausting and stressful, but I am glad I did it. I felt comforted that Ms. McCluskey and

Dr. Bland had heard me. I was proud of myself, perhaps for the first time since the abuse happened.

I was pleased to receive Ms. McCluskey's letter dated September 5, with the draft report of our meeting. It demonstrated to me that the archdiocese was taking my allegations seriously, and that fact alone made me feel better. By September 18, her final report was complete. It completed my fourth act of recovery, with still more to come.

ACT OF RECOVERY

Dr. Conviser

At the August 24 meeting, Dr. Bland had highlighted some of the ways the Archdiocese Office of Assistance Ministry could help survivors of clerical sexual abuse. He said that if I felt it would be helpful to me I would be referred to a psychologist, and the Archdiocese would pay for it. He briefly went on to explain how the process works.

I could choose any psychologist I wanted, but he or she must be licensed in the State of Illinois. The Archdiocese does not interfere with the therapeutic process and is totally hands off. This means any topics discussed with a psychologist can never be used to process claims with the Review Board or by the archdiocesan attorneys. Also, he stated, I could go to this counseling for as long as I needed to, without regard to the cost.

While he was telling me this, I was trying my best to be gracious and to smile. I had way too much on my plate already. I just wanted to get through the meeting. At that point, I had not even thought about seeking counseling. I thanked Dr. Bland for his offer, but I said "No, I will be fine." But he continued on, telling me again there were no strings attached, except that after a year of counseling the psychologist would be contacted by the archdiocese to give them a basic status report on my progress. No therapeutic details would be revealed, only general issues related to making progress towards recovery. All of that sounded reasonable to me, but one idea popped into my head and I could not let it go: I could not believe that people actually attended counseling for a year or more! Again, I thanked Dr. Bland, thinking there was no way I was going to do such a thing. I told him I was way too busy and, besides, I knew I would be fine now that I had told my story to the appropriate people.

Of course I was deluding myself. I was glad I had told my story. I was comforted knowing Dr. Bland and Ms. McCluskey were taking it seriously. After the flurry of activity of telling Kathy and Fr. Greg and hiring Sam Bell and keeping the appointment with the archdiocese, however, I found that I had been left with total heartbreak, pain, and sadness. Yet I was uneasy about asking for any kind of help.

I called Dr. Bland back about one month or so after the

meeting. I was terribly nervous about asking for help, because I had thought I was strong enough to handle anything: the pain and anguish, the sleepless nights, the burden, the sadness. But I was having serious trouble. Kathy and Fr. Greg encouraged me to seek the help that was being offered.

Dr. Bland couldn't have been better about it. He put me at ease, asking only a few basic questions related to what would be convenient times and locations for me. He said he would think about the right referral and get back to me within a day or two. He called later and gave me the name and number of a psychologist, Dr. Jenny Conviser.

I thought I was strong enough to handle anything, but I was having serious trouble.

I was very anxious when I called her to make my first appointment. She asked me a very simple question related to what were we going to be talking about. I stammered my response, unprepared to answer her question. I wasn't yet ready to say to this person I had never met that I had been sexually abused as a child by a priest. I merely stated that Dr. Bland had referred me to her, thinking that she would know that the call must be related to childhood abuse. Of course she did know this, but she wanted to me say it. So she asked politely in another way. I gave her another very awkward, almost unintelligible answer. We made the appointment for the next week.

I began counseling with Dr. Conviser on September 21, 2006, just three months after I initially recovered my memory of the abuse and told Kathy, about one month after my meeting with the archdiocesan officials. I look back with fondness and gratitude now for the time I spent in counseling. I saw Dr. Conviser for close to four years, but beginning the journey was tough for me.

During my first appointment, I did finally articulate that I had been sexually abused repeatedly by a Catholic priest over a four-year period starting when I was 12 years old. Dr. Conviser then asked, "Why are you telling this story now?" I did not know how to answer that question at the time, but it is a great question, and I think I have my answer now.

"Why are you telling me this story now?"

When I recovered my memory of the abuse, I was in a great place in my life at the time. Kathy and I loved each other and our children and the home we had made together. We had great friends. Our kids were healthy, doing well in school, had lots of friends, were playing sports and enjoying life. My company was going along well. I enjoyed developing new business clients and servicing the ones I had. We had prepared for the education of our kids and already had some retirement money put aside. I was healthy and exercising and feeling good, and so was Kathy. We were both involved at our parish and felt happy and fulfilled. I believe it was because I was in that safe environment that I was able to let my guard down. So, upon reading the June 14 *Chicago Tribune* article about my abuser, I no longer needed to suppress the memories of his abuse and could finally discover for myself that what I endured at the hands of my abuser was not normal behavior but in fact something that was traumatic, sinful, and criminal.

By fully realizing I had lost my own innocent childhood to satisfy the sexual needs of a perverse and depraved man, I finally recognized and admitted that I needed psychological help. In the early weeks of counseling, however, I was sure I could "get over it" quickly and move on. I thought if I did not dwell on the pain and stayed focused on the good aspects of my life, I would be fine.

It took me some time, and a lot of help from Dr. Conviser, to fully appreciate all the things I had lost in my life because of what that man did to me. My abuser had been friends with my parents. He used this relationship to manipulate them so they would trust him, so there wouldn't be any questions asked when the invitation came to have me and a few other boys come up to his room in the rectory for pizza. Yes, when I went up to his room, often there was pizza to eat, but there was so much more stuff that was truly disgusting to me then, and now.

Several times during counseling, the topic of my parents came up. Each and every time I decided not to tell them. My parents are older, still alive and in good health. We have a good relationship, and I love them. I decided I would never want to visit upon them the pain and suffering that would come if I told them the truth about my abuser. I knew deep inside I must tell them, but at that point the issue remained unresolved. As a grown man with children of my own, whom my wife and I wished to protect and keep safe from any harm, I initially thought I would be totally devastated if I ever found out my children had been sexually abused by a trusted family friend. I know now that I would want them to tell me right away. But at that point I wanted to protect my parents from this knowledge as I had my entire life. It remained an issue in my counseling.

Throughout counseling, and still today as I think of the abuse that happened to me as a child, I immediately looked to my children, Colleen and Michael. As I write this, Colleen is 16 and Michael is 14 years old. By the time I was the same age, I had been sexually abused for years.

Entering counseling and sticking with it was my fifth act of recovery. The next was meeting with other survivors, others who had been abused by priests.

ACT OF RECOVERY

The Retreat

The fall of 2006 was a very busy and emotional time for me. In early October, I received the final Review Board Report. I was asked to sign a copy and return it to Leah McCluskey as soon as I could, in the interests of expediting the process. I did so. I was happy everything seemed to be moving along smoothly.

In addition to beginning counseling with Dr. Jenny Conviser (which I had done with the support of both Kathy and the archdiocese), I was also invited to attend a clergy abuse survivors retreat sponsored by the Archdiocese of Chicago Office of Assistance Ministry. Dr. Michael Bland, the same man who was at my interview, had invited me and other clergy abuse survivors to a weekend retreat. When he asked me, I immediately said I would go, but as the date came closer, I became very anxious. To my knowledge, I had never met other adult survivors of childhood sexual abuse.

I worried about what it was going to be like to meet other survivors. Was I going to meet someone there I knew as a child? Or another person abused by my priest abuser? I imagined such an experience would be too difficult and painful for me to bear. During each workday, and at home, I was physically and emotionally exhausted from the stress. Telling my story to the archdiocesan officials, on-going weekly counseling, and now this retreat — I felt everything was moving too fast and getting too complicated.

I felt everything was moving too fast.

The day before the retreat was a typical workday for me, but I felt things were spinning out of control. In desperation, I called my good friend Frank Vance on his cell phone. We had known each other since our family moved into the neighborhood years before, and he and I had become friends right away. Our kids were in the same classes and were also friends. Frank is someone I look up to, and for some reason I felt I could talk with him about the retreat.

Frank picked up as he was driving to the airport for a business trip. I asked him if he had a moment to talk. Then I told him, right there on the phone, about being abused as a child. I was fully crying now. I told Frank I had told Kathy, Fr. Greg, and officials at the archdiocese, and that the next day I was going on this survivors retreat and was going to meet other survivors of clergy abuse. I told him I was scared.

The first thing Frank said in reply was, "Thank you Mike for telling me." I was immediately relieved. I had taken a risk, a big risk, in telling Frank my story of abuse, especially on the phone. I had feared that another guy might not understand why I had not fought back harder. I was afraid he might think less of me in some way. But Frank went on to say he felt I was doing a courageous thing in trying to come to terms with my past. He encouraged me not to worry so much about the retreat and said he would say a prayer for me during the weekend. His voice was calming, and my anxiety dissipated.

I thanked Frank for listening and for being my friend.

I did go on the retreat the next day. I was greeted warmly by Dr. Bland and by Dr. Paul Ashton, who was leading the retreat. I was introduced to other men and women who had been abused by clerics. Each person's story of abuse was deeply personal, heart-wrenching, and difficult to hear, but listening to each story I realized that, although the details differed, the stories had similar elements: trusting deeply religious parents; a charismatic, funny, seemingly kind priest; and a young boy or girl who idolized and revered the man who would abuse them.

I discovered on that retreat that when you talked with others who had experienced abuse during the most tender, innocent, and sweet time of their childhood, and you spoke with them of the profound and totally devastating lifelong effects of betrayal by a priest or religious person, you became so close to them that you became soul mates. Those conversations remain sacred to me. They were difficult to endure, but I'm glad I participated.

There was a moment of catharsis for me in telling my story to others and in listening to their stories. It is difficult to know exactly when I began to feel less anxious about what had happened to me, but as I think back I must say it was the moment I walked through the door of the retreat house to begin that weekend.

Several archdiocesan officials joined us for parts of the retreat. This was important to me in a different way, because it showed me that the concern being shown for the survivors of abuse was not just at the staff level but went right to the top. Jimmy Lago, the lay Chancellor of the archdiocese, two auxiliary bishops, and Cardinal Francis George all came and listened to our stories of abuse and betrayal and answered our questions directly and honestly. I was glad they stayed and spent considerable time with us. They got to hear some very difficult stories. Having them there certainly didn't make the Church's initial failure to respond to the clergy sexual abuse crisis acceptable, but I was left with the definite feeling that they cared about us and were sorry these heinous crimes had happened to us at the hands of a priest. I felt they were trying to take the corrective action necessary to prevent abusive priests from ever harming children again. I also believed they truly wanted to help us heal from what had been inflicted on us in any way they could.

I came home from the retreat and, after speaking with Kathy about it all, called Frank Vance. We talked face-to-face for some time. The entire retreat experience, including connecting with Frank, was my sixth act of recovery. I would soon experience my next, which would take me into the world of the lawyers.

In December, I received another letter from the Review Board. In the letter, Ms. McCluskey stated that at their past meeting the Review Board discussed the account of my abuse and felt there was cause to continue. They asked if I had any additional information I wished to provide. I was thankful for this letter and pleased with the openness and full disclosure of the process. It made me feel better knowing Church officials were moving forward with my case. I responded to Ms. McCluskey's request by saying I had no other information to offer. I didn't. They had it all.

I had it in writing that the Review Board believed me!

On January 30, 2007, I received a letter from the Review Board that gave me great comfort and relief. Five months from my initial meeting with archdiocese officials, I had it in writing that they believed me!

When I was 12 years old, I could not have imagined that anybody — not my parents and certainly not Church officials

— would believe the bad things that my abuser had done and was doing to me. When I was a child, I thought everyone in my life would blame me for questioning the character of a priest and tell me I was making it all up. I feared I would be the one who would be punished if I said anything. That is the insidious nature of the sexual abuse of minors, especially when its perpetrator is a sick and evil priest who has been put in a position of power and respect and then believed and protected by those who put him there.

I have to admit that I carried some of those same feelings with me as an adult. With the letter from the archdiocese in hand, however, I could no longer feel that way. I had spoken up. They had listened to and heard my story and had believed me — not "him." I cried and cried and cried with the letter in my hand. It meant I could now continue the healing process. The healing did not come right away, and I realize that it must continue for the rest of my life, but a great emotional, psychological, and spiritual burden had been lifted from my shoulders. An indescribable feeling of relief had been given to me. In writing.

ACT OF RECOVERY

Mayra Flores
and Jim Serritella

I had to get a new attorney, Timothy Mahoney, to handle the
financial settlement with the archdiocese. The negotiations
were out of Sam Bell's area of expertise. Letters were exchanged
between Tim and the attorneys for the Archdiocese of Chicago.
I wanted to settle my claim for damages with the archdiocese
without going to court, and both sides agreed to use a
mediator. We set a date of October 30, 2007. In preparation
for our mediation date, I saw a forensic psychiatrist, Dr. Lyle
Rossiter, Jr., a specialist who could determine the extent of
the psychological and emotional damages I had endured and
estimate approximate costs of treatment over time.

This experience was emotionally disruptive. It was Dr. Rossiter's job to dig deep into my memories. I told him about my relationship with my parents, my home life as a child, and my relationship with them now. I talked about how religious they were and how that had affected me. I recalled the acts of abuse and how the priest was able to perpetrate the abuse over time. I described the abuser's high standing in the community, how he was a figure beloved by many people — including my parents. The psychiatrist asked about my relationship with my wife and kids and even my brother and sister.

Recounting and labeling these specific memories and feelings was extremely stressful for me. Dr. Rossiter spoke with my wife too. He asked her if I had disrupted sleep, if I had lost weight and how much, if I was distracted at home with her and the kids, and more.

The psychiatrist took copious notes and produced a report, dated October 24, 2007. For me, the most important passage was this: "Mr. Hoffman's adolescent growth and development, as well as his relationships with his parents, siblings, and peers, were profoundly affected by (the abuser's) violations of him. The overall trauma of the abuse involves not just the effects of the acts themselves but also Mr. Hoffman's feelings of disillusionment with and betrayal by a man who was idealized and revered by him and his family and by numerous other parishioners. Because adolescence is an era in which idealized figures are especially important, (the abuser's) betrayal was and has remained particularly traumatic."

To me, this quote provided an objective statement of the complete and total devastation that occurred when this priest betrayed me, my family, and the larger parish family. Certain aspects of my story were verified during Dr. Rossiter's conversation with Kathy. The report finished with his conclusions. My attorney and I took this report with us to mediation the following week.

The law offices of Burke, Warren, McKay, and Serritella are on the 22nd floor of IBM Plaza in Chicago. The firm was (and continues to be) the lead outside legal counsel for the Archdiocese of Chicago. I met my attorney in the lobby of the building. I felt ill. I had not slept well the night before. I was unsure what would happen up there and didn't know how it was all going to end. I was also having second thoughts. I didn't have much to say to my attorney. We entered the elevator and pushed the button. The elevator opened into a beautiful lobby, and I immediately felt intimidated and overwhelmed. I had never been in any place like that before. But we were greeted warmly by the receptionist, and since we were early we were escorted to a small meeting room. I was glad. I needed some time to calm myself.

I was having second thoughts.

I had always feared that the attorneys for the archdiocese — in trying to protect their client's interests — would be the ones to try to discredit me, question my character, or imply the abuse I endured wasn't that bad. I figured any attorney would do that. If that happened, I expected I would react with resentment and anger.

Within a few minutes, a woman named Mayra Flores knocked on the door to our meeting room. Ms. Flores is the Assistant Director of the Office of Assistance Ministry for the Archdiocese of Chicago. She and her Director, Matt Hunicutt, reach out to the survivors of clergy sexual abuse and their families.

I had met Ms. Flores during the Review Board process and liked her. I was happy she was there. Her presence was somehow very comforting to me. She stated they were ready to go in the main conference room and escorted us down the hallway, my attorney leading the way. I hung back with her as if to a life preserver. She asked if I was OK. I didn't respond, because I wasn't OK. By this time my attorney had already entered the room, but I held the door for Ms. Flores and asked her to enter first. The fact is I didn't want to enter the room at all. When I finally did, I saw handshakes being exchanged across the great conference room table. I didn't feel comfortable doing that, so I walked around the table to shake hands with the firm's lead attorney for the case, Jim Serritella. My attorney asked me to return to our side of the table. The situation was awkward all around.

Introductions were made. Ms. Flores began the meeting by telling everyone in the room about the services of her office. Addressing me directly, she stated that Cardinal George would make himself available to meet with me individually (as he offers to do with all clergy-abuse survivors) if I ever felt that would help my recovery. I thanked her and said I was indeed interested in speaking with him. She noted this and then excused herself from the room.

The opening statement by Tim Mahoney was a powerful recounting of the effects of abuse in my life. He described the feelings of shame and humiliation I had experienced in coming forward to tell my story. He listed the acts of abuse made upon me by the particular priest in question and stated that the archdiocese knew or should have known that such abuse was occurring in the rectory on church grounds. He referred to the report written by the forensic psychiatrist about the long-term effects of the abuse I had endured. He concluded his remarks by asking the archdiocese to compensate me for the damages I had suffered and continued to suffer.

Mr. Serritella began his remarks by addressing me directly. He apologized for the abuse by a priest whom they now knew was a very bad man. I was immediately relieved to hear this. The lead outside attorney believed me! He would not re-victimize me by character assassination like they did on TV. He continued to say they were here simply to help victims of clergy abuse in the recovery process.

My attorney and I were then asked to go to another small conference room. A mediator then went between each conference room to express the issues for either side. Beyond describing the acts of abuse to them again, I wanted them to admit that an employee of the Church should not be allowed to hurt young children like I was hurt. And if the Church in any way knew about or allowed this kind of abuse to happen, the Church itself should feel some real punishment.

In terms of individual, concrete damages that could have been considered for "compensation," I had virtually none. (This, by the way, is not true of a lot of survivors of sexual abuse.) I am happily married with two well-adjusted children, run a successful company, and am in excellent health. In short, I do not have any obvious damages — on the surface. I do suffer from deep emotional scarring, and there is no compensation for that other than knowing I have been able to tell my story and hoping I can make a difference in the lives of others.

With tears in my eyes, I accepted his apology.

Many ideas were expressed from room to room by the excellent mediator. Finally a settlement amount was agreed upon that to me felt just. It seemed to be large enough that the archdiocese would feel the effects of allowing one of its priests to harm children, enough to encourage it to take corrective action to prevent it from happening again.

We were asked to rejoin the attorneys from the archdiocese back in the main conference room. There, the mediator announced that an agreement had been reached. Standing next to me was Jim Serritella. He immediately reached out for my hand with both of his hands and said again how sorry he was for what happened to me as a boy. With tears in my eyes, I accepted his apology. The day had been a day of emotional upheaval and unrest. I was exhausted.

Jim Serritella then did something I will never forget. His family lives in Queen of All Saints parish, just next to our parish of St. Mary of the Woods on the northwest side of Chicago. Mr. Serritella asked me if I knew a certain family in our neighborhood. In fact, I had coached one of the sons in baseball. We then made pleasant conversation for a few moments about our mutual friends. On one of the most difficult days in my life — after facing the attorneys for the Archdiocese of Chicago and standing up to them and telling my story of abuse and its effects on me and my family — my lasting memory was about the normalcy and decency of just talking with a neighbor about someone we both knew.

It was the simple human concern shown to me by Ms. Flores and Mr. Serritella that day — not the financial settlement with the archdiocese — that became my seventh act of recovery. The next one would be one of the hardest.

Tim Mahoney and I departed from the 22nd floor. We were speechless in the elevator. We walked in the lobby for some time and remained silent. I think he was waiting for me to say something, but I didn't know what to say. I was unsettled. I simply didn't know how I felt. Finally, I thanked him for all of his efforts on my behalf. He left for his car and I for mine.

I didn't know what to do or where to go. I didn't want to go back to work and was not ready to go back home. I drove to Navy Pier, a place I love to hang out. I walked the entire length of the pier four times. It was a warm, fall afternoon. After some time, I sat on a bench and watched the people passing by. Finally, I called Kathy. I told her it was done, that we had settled. Again, we were both silent on the phone for a few moments. She asked me where I was. I told her I was sitting at Navy Pier. She said gently, "Why don't you come home, Mike?" I said OK and went home. That's when I started to cry — almost the whole way home. I cannot really describe any specific feelings I had, just that I cried. Hard.

ACTS OF RECOVERY

Mom and Dad

The very next morning was Saturday. I knew what I had to do.
I picked up the phone and called my parents, and I told them
about the abuse I had suffered at the hands of our priest when I
was a child. I had been holding this information from them for
so long, but I realized I didn't have the will to do it anymore.

The anguished cries of my mother were almost easier to
take than my father's almost completely inaudible mumbles.
I knew Mom could identify and label her emotions and Dad
could not. I told them about telling Kathy and Fr. Greg, about
coming forward to the archdiocese and going through the
Review Board process and reaching a settlement. But mostly, I

told them about holding back the pain and sadness for so long that — even though I still didn't want to tell them — I had to. We all cried and cried and cried on the phone, until I couldn't take it anymore. I apologized for causing them pain and told them I had to end the call.

My parents called me back the next day. My mom was the first on the phone. She thanked me for telling them about the abuse. We talked about the difficult times in our family back then. The abuse and how it had affected me as a 12-year-old boy and the cumulative impact of deceit and betrayal my abuser had on our family dynamic could not be overstated. We had been a terribly dysfunctional family at the time, and my abuse at the hands of what my parents thought was a family friend was part of the reason. Mom said that now we knew about it we could begin to heal from it.

We cried until I couldn't take it anymore.

My dad agreed with us, but he was mostly listening. I felt bad about visiting this kind of painful burden on my parents in their old age. After this call, my heart ached especially for Dad, because I knew he would blame himself. Just knowing Mom, I knew she would be able to rise above it all.

As I worried about Dad, I thought about one of my fondest memories as a child. It was back in 1977, when I was 12 and he and I went to see the movie *Star Wars: A New Hope.* Reflecting on this memory, I decided to send Dad a gift for his upcoming birthday. I was so excited about this idea that I ordered one for myself as well: Hammacher Schlemmer sells a Luke Skywalker replica lightsaber, complete with movie action sounds. It had the look and feel of a real lightsaber! I shipped his directly to his home. The large box came a few days prior to his birthday. I had never sent a gift like this to him before. He was curious, just like a kid. He called me to ask if he could open it up prior to his birthday. I laughed, but I asked him to wait.

The anticipation was too great, however, so Dad opened up the box two days before his birthday. He was happy to know that I remembered the good times when I was young. I told him I considered the day we saw *Star Wars* my "perfect day," a day of sweetness and innocence, the joy of a son spending time with his father.

Finally telling my parents about the abuse I had endured as a child from a priest-friend of theirs was my eighth act of recovery. There would be more, but beginning to remember and celebrate the good times I did have when I was young has led to real healing and reconciliation for my family.

ACT OF RECOVERY

Cardinal George

A week or so after the mediation, I received a call from Mayra Flores asking about a time to meet with Cardinal Francis George. She suggested a few dates and times that had already been allocated for this on the Cardinal's calendar. We agreed on a date during the third week of December. I was impressed it was going to happen so quickly.

As we approached the date, however, I realized I did not want to go alone. Kathy works at our parish school and had the kindergarten Christmas pageant that day, which I didn't want her to miss. She suggested I call her father, Bill Powers. He would go with me. I thought that was a great idea.

With that issue settled, I had to put some thought into what I wanted to say to Cardinal George. I was thinking a lot about my parents and how my siblings and I had been raised, and so I went to look at one of our old family photo albums. I was leafing through the pages with no specific purpose, just reflecting on my past, when I saw photos of my abuser at a family party in our basement with the rest of our family. This was an unexpected but important reminder that my abuser was a dear friend to my parents. He not only abused me to satisfy his sexual desires, he betrayed my parents' friendship and affection in the most profound and devastating way. I took these photos out of the photo album so I could show them to Cardinal George.

The morning I met Cardinal George was another surreal day in a string of surreal days. I didn't sleep well the night before, and I didn't say much to Kathy and the kids as they headed off for the Christmas pageant. My father-in-law came to the door dressed in a sport coat. I was wearing a business suit. We began our drive to the Cardinal's residence. Bill sensed my unease and tried to make conversation. I appreciated his effort, and on any other day I would have been very talkative, but on this day I was preoccupied with what I was going to say and how it was all going to go.

We arrived at the Cardinal's residence a few minutes before our scheduled meeting time. Bill slowed the car as we approached the old mansion that had been the home of Chicago's archbishops for decades. Bill drove slowly around the semi-circle drive that passed the front of the house, then parked along the side. He stopped and, with the car still running, we stared at the house in silence. My father-in-law has a dry sense of humor, and after a few seconds he broke the silence by suggesting we could turn around and go home. I smiled at him, knowing he was kidding. But it had crossed my mind.

We walked around to the front door and rang the bell. After only a moment, the door opened a crack and one of the Sisters of Mercy, the order of nuns who care for the home and provide for the Cardinal, answered the door and asked, "How can I help you?" I responded by saying, "My name is Mike Hoffman and I have an appointment with Cardinal George." She replied, "Yes, you do, Mr. Hoffman. Please come in." She opened the door wide, and standing in the hallway was Mayra Flores, the woman from the archdiocese who had been so kind to me before the mediation. She had come there just to make sure I was OK. She gave me a big hug and shook hands with Bill. I was so relieved she was there.

My father-in-law suggested we could turn around and go home.

It was the Christmas season, and the Cardinal's home was decorated beautifully. Mayra, Bill, and I sat near the Christmas tree for a few minutes in conversation. Then we heard Cardinal George descending the staircase. I knew it was him because he has a pronounced limp because of childhood polio. I realized I could hear my heart beating loudly in my chest. I wondered if he could hear it?

I was not anxious about meeting with the Cardinal as an individual. I was anxious about meeting his "office" — what his office represented to me as a practicing Catholic and in terms of the abuse I had suffered at the hands of one of the archdiocesan priests when I was a young boy.

Cardinal George immediately shook my hand and thanked me for coming. I introduced him to my father-in-law, Bill, and congratulated him on his recent election as the President of the United States Conference of Catholic Bishops. He was gracious and friendly. Almost immediately he asked if we should meet as a group or if I wished to meet with him in private. I told him I preferred to meet him in private. I felt that this was something I had to do alone. So he and I proceeded to the Mundelein Room, a beautiful sitting room on the first floor, while Bill and Mayra remained seated by the Christmas tree.

His Eminence and I speak for close to 45 minutes. I had brought with me the photos of my abuser at our family party in our basement and gave them to him to look at. I spoke about my parents and our upbringing. I told him my abuser had been a dear friend to my parents and about the ceramic paten and chalice they had given him that he used at Mass. I told the Cardinal that this man not only had abused me to satisfy his own sexual urges, he had betrayed my parents' trust. I told the Cardinal that the cumulative effect of the manipulation, lies, repeated violations, and perverse actions of one of his priests was like a wedge being pounded into the heart of each of my family members.

The Cardinal listened very carefully to me. He asked about my parents and my brother and sister. I told him each of them struggled with sadness, pain, and heartache for what our family had lost. I went on to say I had been treated well and with respect and dignity by the Review Board and the outside attorneys for the archdiocese. He was genuinely glad about that. I talked about my wife Kathy and how supportive she had been to me throughout the ordeal. I also talked about our kids, Colleen and Michael, and how I realized I could not protect them from all the harm that might come to them in their lives, but that my heart would break if they were ever sexually abused the way I was.

The Cardinal listened very carefully.

I believe Cardinal George heard me and understood the depth of my feelings. I felt I had said all I wanted say to him. He apologized to me for the abuse I had endured and the effect it had on me and my family. I accepted his apology. It was my ninth act of recovery. Cardinal George would be involved in the next two as well.

As we stood to depart, I realized I was exhausted. The Cardinal seemed tired as well. We met Bill and Mayra, who were still engaged in lively conversation. They seemed to truly enjoy one another's company. I was somehow comforted to see that. After we all had a few more minutes of conversation about the history of the home, I thanked Cardinal George and Mayra Flores for their time. When Bill and I were back in the car, both of us let out a big sigh of relief simultaneously, which caused us both to smile.

ACT OF RECOVERY

The Healing Garden

In a very short amount of time, I had reached a settlement with the Archdiocese of Chicago, finally told my parents my story of being abused, and met with the leader of our Church, Cardinal George. Each of those events individually should have required some time to process, but I took them on all at once. I didn't plan it that way. It just happened.

Because of my physical and emotional exhaustion, I realized I needed more help. I continued the individual counseling with Dr. Conviser for some time, and eventually I began to feel calmed. My heart was at peace with all I had done. In fact, I was proud of myself.

Soon thereafter, I sensed that after going through all I had been through, I could not simply go back to life as it was before I came forward with my story. This story, and its effects, is now a normal, integral part of who I am. I realized I had been changed, and I began looking for something to do to make life better for other survivors. I found it difficult to put my finger on specifically what I wanted to do. Looking for answers, but with no specific direction or purpose, I wrote Cardinal George a letter.

I did this as an act of faith. I believe the sexual abuse of children by certain members of the clergy, and the way in which those crimes have been handled — not only in Chicago but around the world — has not only profoundly affected survivors and their families but also wounded our larger Church. I wondered in my letter to the Cardinal if there was something I could do beyond individual counseling that might help continue to heal my own wounds and also help others.

I could not simply go back to life as it was before.

A couple weeks after I sent the letter, I received a call from Matt Hunnicut, the director of the Office of Assistance Ministry for the archdiocese. He mentioned the Cardinal had received my letter, and we talked about it for a while. Again, with no specific purpose or goal in mind, I asked him if an appointment with the Cardinal could be arranged. He said he would check and see. After some time, he confirmed an appointment for December, 2008, almost a year after I had met with the Cardinal. Prior to the appointment, Mr. Hunnicut and I had several more conversations. During this time, the Diocese of Oakland in California had opened their new cathedral, called Christ the Light. On the grounds of the cathedral they had installed a "healing garden" dedicated to the victims of clergy sexual abuse within that diocese. The two of us read the newspaper articles and talked about this idea for Chicago. The date for my appointment with the Cardinal was drawing near.

On a cold, snowy day in December, Mr. Hunnicut and I met with Cardinal George in his office at the Archdiocese Pastoral Center. Inspired simply by my faith-filled desire to open up a dialogue with the Cardinal about healing my own wounds of abuse beyond counseling, the three of us discussed a wide range of topics. In my heart I knew I was not alone among survivors in my pain, sadness, and heartache. I was aware of the depth of the pain the abuse had caused in my family, and I assumed it had done so in many others. I still had no specific idea to present to the Cardinal, but as we continued talking our conversation settled on the creation of a healing garden in Chicago. The Cardinal agreed a committee should be formed to look at the idea and report back to him. This sounded great to both Mr. Hunnicut and me, and we thanked the Cardinal for taking the time to talk with us.

I didn't know what to expect, but right away, in January, 2009, a committee was formed with four clergy abuse survivors, two diocesan priests, and four staff members from the Office for the Protection of Children and Youth of the Archdiocese of Chicago. I was personally energized by this idea and the enthusiasm of the other committee members. To me, just the effort to gather abuse survivors, priests, and archdiocesan staff with widely different points of view on the subject of clergy abuse and how to heal from it was an experience I will never forget. As our committee process got underway, I was happy to have something concrete to focus on other than myself. This project fit in with my realization that I could not go back to my prior life.

Working on this project helped me normalize the years of holding back my story. I told more of our friends: Pat and Christina, Mitch and Laura, Brian and Marlene. For over 30 years it had been painful to me to refrain from talking with friends about my youth because something held me back. Now I knew what that something was, and once I got it out in the open I could join with others in telling other, happier, stories from my youth.

During this time, working with our planning committee, I felt I could be myself in social settings with family and friends. I became involved with a support group of childhood abuse survivors and phased out of individual counseling with Dr. Conviser. The support group was made up of men and women who had been abused by family members. I was the only clergy-abuse survivor. I will never describe what was said in our group meetings, as those conversations are sacred to me, but I will say I learned about courage, compassion, hope, and despair. I heard stories similar to my own, about how an adult can manipulate others to create situations with children that will satisfy their sexual desires. I learned about the survival skills of other victims and how they coped with family and friends. I no longer participate in the support group, but I think about them often. I carry their stories with me to this day. I am motivated by what was said and hope it will help me make a difference on the issue of preventing child abuse and protecting children.

Our healing garden planning committee presented a plan to the Cardinal, and he approved it immediately. Major funding of the garden was made possible from gifts from religious orders, some of whom had also harbored pedophiles in their ranks. My wife and I and our family and friends contributed money. Other benefactors, some anonymous, made donations as well. Soon, the archdiocese assigned a project manager. I was fascinated by this man. His name was Jim Vodak. His presence made the entire experience real for me. Mr. Vodak asked me if I wanted to attend the project management meetings as the construction got underway, and also invited me to the weekly meetings that happened during construction. I never missed a meeting. It was a fulfilling experience for me to see the project take shape and work with an archdiocese staff that was committed to making the healing garden a reality. I considered it a rare privilege to be able to witness the dedication of the various interests within

I carry their stories with me to this day.

the Archdiocese of Chicago to create a beautiful space as a place of healing for all childhood abuse victims and their families. I would eat lunch in my car watching the workers. It made me feel good to see the progress being made each day.

Today the foliage in the garden exhibits vibrant colors and various textures throughout the year. The plants are hardy, and as they grow and mature they will provide shade. In the heart of the city of Chicago, the healing garden is a calming place to relax, reflect, and feel the presence of God in nature. In addition, the committee felt all visitors to the healing garden should be inspired and informed about healing from the tragic effects of childhood sexual abuse in our society and in the Church.

The healing garden is situated right in the middle of a now vacated city street, right next to Holy Family Church on Roosevelt Road, in plain view for all to see. Approaching the Garden, any visitor will see a beautiful bronze sculpture of Jesus, Mary, and Joseph joyfully dancing in a circle at the center of the garden. As you enter, you see two plaques. The first is a personal quote from Cardinal George. The Cardinal is first and foremost our pastor, and our committee agreed it would be healing and helpful to have this personal reflection by him inscribed on a plaque:

A path in a beautiful garden leads to healing and peace.
In offering this path, the Church offers as well
a profound apology to those
who have been sexually abused
by priests or others in the Archdiocese of Chicago.

The path of their suffering is one that must be trod by all,
so that all, together, might find that peace
which is the gift of God.

Jesus accompanies everyone on the path of life,
and he is the heart of this healing garden.

The second plaque contains our planning committee vision statement. The abuse survivors on our committee felt strongly about identifying ourselves as clergy-abuse survivors who were attempting to reach out to anyone who might be suffering from any form of abuse or other tragic event. We hoped that our little garden might help them heal from the pain and sadness of their heartache:

The creation of this healing garden is an attempt by us,
clergy abuse survivors of the Archdiocese of Chicago,
to heal, learn and grow from the physical, mental,
emotional and spiritual harm done to us.

*We wish to reach out to you who may have suffered
from any tragic event that has left your hearts broken,
just like ours.*

*Together in this healing space,
may we find within ourselves a place to feel free:
free from fear, free from shame and free from judgment.*

On the center pathway of the garden is the 600-pound bronze sculpture of the Holy Family. Mary, Joseph, and a youthful Jesus are shown joyfully dancing in a circle. The sculpture is called "The Circle of Love" and was created by artist George Michael Meyers of Prescott, Arizona. Our committee believed that the sacred bonds between parent and child are often broken when a child is abused.

Joy and happiness had been torn away from me and now I wanted it back.

I know this to be true in my personal life. I believe I have been on a difficult journey since I was a 12-year-old boy, a journey to reclaim the family relationships that had been lost to abuse. The joyous depiction of Jesus in a loving and safe place with his mother and father is a great inspiration to me and to others on the committee. I had that kind of joy and happiness when I was a child. It had been torn away from me and my family by a very bad man who was our priest at the time. Now I wanted it back.

Next to the sculpture, which was donated by the Sisters of the Holy Family of Nazareth, you will find a prayer to bless and protect all families, offered to us by the sisters. You can sit on a bench facing the sculpture to reflect and pray:

O Holy Family Jesus, Mary and Joseph,
bless and protect all the families of the world and safeguard their
unity, fidelity, integrity and dignity.

Enable them to live according to God's law
that they may fulfill their sublime vocation.

May their lives be a reflection of yours
and may they enjoy your presence forever in heaven.

Continuing to walk on the central path, you will find another plaque with a quote from the USCCB Dallas Charter regarding the "Ministry of Reconciliation":

We feel a particular responsibility for the "ministry of
reconciliation" (2 Corinthians 5:18) which God,
who reconciled us to himself through Christ, has given us.

The love of Christ impels us to ask forgiveness
for our own faults but also to appeal to all—to those
who have been victimized, to those who have offended,

and to all who have felt the wound of this scandal—to be
reconciled to God and one another.

The last quote was offered to our committee by a survivor of clergy abuse and as an aid to his own healing:

There is hope for a tree that has been cut down;
it can come back to life and sprout.

Even though its roots grow old,
and its stump dies on the ground,
with water it will sprout like a young plant
(Book of Job 14:7-9).

The Healing Garden of the Archdiocese of Chicago was dedicated on June 9, 2011, in a beautiful prayer service and dedication event attended by over 300 people. My wife, Kathy, and our kids, Colleen and Michael, were with me. My father-in-law Bill and others from Kathy's side of the family came to share the day with us. I was also surrounded by many friends. I was thankful for such love and support.

Working on the healing garden project and seeing it become a beautiful reality was my 10th act of recovery.

ACT OF RECOVERY

Mass of Atonement and Hope

On September 11, 2012, Cardinal George commemorated the 10-year anniversary of the Dallas Charter for the Protection of Children and Young People with a Mass and a social in the Healing Garden of the Archdiocese of Chicago. Our planning committee of abuse survivors, priests, and staff remained together, and we were involved in the planning of this Mass of Atonement and Hope. When I found out the date of this event, I called my parents to see if they could attend. Yes, they were free and were happy to come to visit with us and attend this special Mass.

At this time, it had been six years since I first told my

wife, Kathy, that I had been sexually abused as a boy. Since then I had been working on how to reconcile myself to the abuse I endured and the effect it had on my family. Attending this Mass with my family was my 11th act of recovery.

I love my parents. As a boy, I would wait for Dad to come home from work. When he entered the house, I would tell him about my day. He would put his briefcase down, kiss my Mom, then go up to their room to change out of his business suit. I would follow him through the kitchen and up the stairs, still talking. He would change and I followed him down the stairs, still talking. I looked up to him, and I was always so happy when he was home. I wanted to be like him.

My mother was asked to give the first reading from the Book of Lamentations.

Mom loved to talk too. She always expressed strong family values and valued family history. She knew where she came from and she talked about it, and because of that I have a strong identity. One of my fondest memories is of counting all the pennies, nickels, and dimes in my piggy bank. Mom would take me to the bank to make my own deposit. I would fill out a deposit slip to my own passbook savings account; give the bag of coins to the teller; then check to see the increase in my savings, plus interest. Mom taught me the value of consistent work and savings, and I do this with my kids now.

My folks live in the San Francisco Bay area. They traveled

a long way to attend the Mass. My mother was asked to give the first reading. It was from the Book of Lamentations. It is a difficult reading that talks about the despair and isolation felt by someone in exile. The Gospel was read by Cardinal George. It was a beautiful reading of the Beatitudes from St. Matthew.

I sat in the pew of historic Holy Family Church, with my parents sitting next to me and my wife and children behind me, looking for help and guidance. I had worked six long years to find some peace and healing in my heart. My parents had traveled a great distance to be with me. I knew they had suffered from terrible sadness and pain resulting from the knowledge their son had been abused by a trusted priest and friend. They had been betrayed by that man in the most horrific way. I had endured unspeakable pain and heartache because of that abuse, and it had affected my relationship with my brother and sister. In my view, my parents had accepted that burden by coming to the Mass.

The Cardinal's homily was excellent. He spoke about how the juxtaposition of the two readings highlights the balance we all need in our lives. As I listened to him speak, I looked over at my mom, who was listening intently, and then at my dad, who was also focused on the Cardinal. Here we were, laying our terrible heartache, pain, and sadness in front of the beautiful altar at Holy Family Church. I was proud of my parents and happy to be their son.

The Mass concluded with a wonderful social in the healing garden. During this time, Cardinal George had been undergoing chemotherapy treatments for the recurrence of bladder cancer. Despite what I can only imagine were his personal health concerns and exhaustion from the effects of the treatment, his saying the Mass of Atonement and Hope was a moment of healing and reconciliation for me. I never got the chance to personally thank him for saying this Mass and for his commitment to helping to heal, as with all of us in an imperfect way, the wounds of abuse in our Church. In my opinion, he put his heart and soul on the line over the difficult issue of reconciling our overall Church to the tragic and long-lasting effects of childhood abuse.

Your Eminence, thank you. By your work and example, you gave me and my family the opportunity to reclaim what had been lost. You helped the Church admit its sin, ask for forgiveness, and put safeguards in place to try to prevent abuse from happening in the future.

ACT OF RECOVERY

Fr. Mike
and Fr. Pat

Within two weeks after the Mass of Atonement and Hope, I
wrote a short letter to the current pastor of the parish where I
had been abused, Fr. Michael McGovern at the Church of St.
Mary in Lake Forest, Illinois. I copied my current pastor at
St. Mary of the Woods, Fr. Pat Cecil. In the letter, I stated my
Catholic identity had been formed in that parish and, despite
the abuse I endured there, I still considered myself to be blessed
to be a Catholic. In the spirit of healing and reconciliation, I
asked if he would meet with me.

Within a week, I received a letter back from Fr. Mike.
He thanked me for reaching out to him and said he would be

happy to meet with me and Fr. Pat. We traded some dates and finally agreed to a date in November.

I picked up Fr. Pat from the rectory at St. Mary of the Woods early, so we could eat a sandwich before our meeting with Fr. Mike. At lunch, Fr. Pat told me about a dear priest friend of his who, as it turned out, had sexually abused many boys. At the time of this writing, this priest is still serving a prison sentence, and his name and photo are on the Archdiocese of Chicago's list of abusive priests. This was clearly an uncomfortable subject for Fr. Pat, but he felt compelled to tell me. He is aware of the pain and anguish his friend caused the victims and their families, and he said he hoped I would be successful in finding peace and solace. He promised to walk with me along the way. Despite the pain that Fr. Pat suffered regarding the truth that his friend was an abuser, I am happy he told me. I am so happy to have him in my life. Maybe together, with God's grace, we can both heal our wounds.

This was clearly an uncomfortable subject for Fr. Pat.

As we approached the door to the rectory at Church of St. Mary, my heart thumped loud in my chest. I had suffered much emotional stress because of the abuse that had taken place in that building and had held back the stories of what happened there for over 30 years. As a 12-year-old boy, and still even now as a 48-year-old man, it was and still is difficult to label the confusing mix of physical, mental, and spiritual harm done to me there by a very bad man.

Fr. Mike greeted Fr. Pat and me. I still didn't know what I was going to say. Fr. Mike escorted us into a beautiful sitting room and asked if we would like any coffee or water. I accepted a glass of water. There was an awkward silence for a moment, then Fr. Mike began the conversation by welcoming me back to the Church of St. Mary, the place where, as I stated in my letter, my Catholic identity had been formed. I thanked him for seeing us and said that this was the place where, along with my parent's formation, I had developed my strong Catholic identity, which had endured despite the abuse I suffered there.

With that said, I opened up about going to school there. I talked about my parents' active involvement in a wide variety of parish activities from being lectors, sitting on the parish council, and planning and attending many fundraising activities. My mother was involved in the start of the Youth Ministry program and also worked at the school library. I told Fr. Mike my parents had loved it at St. Mary's. They had made great friends with many parishioners and had great parties at our home. Then I told him how they had become friends with the associate pastor at the time. Knowing my parents, this was a natural thing for them to have done, something that flowed from their activity at the church. This priest had been a charismatic man who was fun for them to be around. He had been invited to many dinner parties at our home. They had total and complete trust in him, so when he invited me and other boys up to his room in the rectory for pizza and soda after certain events, they had always encouraged me to go.

I went on to tell Fr. Mike that, yes, there was pizza on the table, but there was a whole lot more. Fr. Mike and Fr. Pat listened to me and were saddened by what they heard. I finished by saying that despite the abuse I had endured in that building, the overwhelming sadness and pain I suffered then, the difficult family relationships with my parents and siblings growing up and even to this day, and the daily anxiety and stress I still experience as I learn to cope with the devastating truth of the abuse and how it affected me and my family, I feel God's grace each and every day and believe in the power of reconciliation. I told Fr. Mike I was there at St. Mary's because I wanted to reconcile myself to these realities. I believed only by this and other acts of recovery could I live a happy and healthy life.

Fr. Mike thanked me for what I had said and apologized for what had happened to me at the hands of a priest in that building. He talked about how the issue cut so close to the heart and soul of both the abuse survivor and every good and faithful priest.

Fr. Mike went on to suggest I was now having a fulfilling experience as a member at St. Mary of the Woods, just as my parents had at Church of St. Mary. I agreed. I am a lector and was the president of the Athletic Board for three years. Kathy volunteers her time assisting with the fundraising events and as a room mom. We attend virtually every fundraising event. My wife and I are happy there. So my parents were my best role models for how volunteering at church could be a fulfilling experience. I was happy talking with Fr. Mike about them.

At the end of our time together, the three of us prayed for healing and reconciliation of individual abuse victims and their families and for the healing of our overall Church. In addition, we prayed for abusers, that they might admit the evil they had done, ask for forgiveness, and receive the grace of God.

In all, our meeting lasted about one hour. I thanked Fr. Mike for the time he gave us. Fr. Pat and I walked out of the building where I had been sexually abused as a young boy. I was happy. Emotionally exhausted, but happy.

I was emotionally exhausted but happy.

Returning to the place where my abuse had occurred allowed me to realize that no matter what evil my abuser had perpetrated, he could no longer harm me or my family. Nor should I allow him to tear apart the memories of the good things my parents, siblings, and I experienced in our parish life.

This realization was my 12th act of recovery. I know there will continue to be many others, but these were the main ones that have helped in my ongoing healing, and I am thankful for each of them.

Epilogue

As one of my ongoing acts of recovery, I volunteer my time to work with others to help raise awareness of child abuse prevention efforts within our Church and society.

On April 12, 2013, four Catholic elementary schools came to the Healing Garden of the Archdiocese of Chicago to participate in a prayer service and plant pinwheels in the garden for child abuse prevention. The pinwheel is the national symbol of child abuse prevention efforts. It represents the joy, innocence, and fun that should be the experience of all children. Activities like this helps break the code of silence that surrounds the issue of child abuse in our society. By raising awareness of child abuse prevention efforts in our Catholic schools and parishes, both children and parents alike can talk about the difficult child safety issues in our society such as physical, sexual, and verbal abuse, as well as the terrible effects of bullies and bullying.

The prayer service and pinwheel planting was a public show of support for providing a happy, healthy, and safe environment for all children. It has been my experience that Cardinal George and his priests and staff of the Archdiocese of Chicago have shown and continue to show leadership and vision in raising awareness of the important efforts to protect children. As a childhood sexual abuse survivor, I am proud to stand with the Cardinal and his people to lend my name and face and voice to assist in these efforts. Working on this project helps me to heal my own wounds of past abuse.

It is my hope that more schools will attend the prayer service and pinwheel planting ceremony each year. A portion of the proceeds from the sale of this book will be used to defray the annual cost of this event and to provide general support for the good work of the Archdiocese of Chicago's Office for the Protection of Children and Youth.

The symbolic gesture of planting pinwheels is designed to show the public that child abuse and neglect happen in every community and encourage each of us to focus on prevention as a part of an overall plan to break the cycle of abuse.

Thank you for reading my story. May God bless you, as God has blessed me. I finished this book on the Feast of the Assumption, one of the major feasts of St. Mary, the patroness of two parishes that have meant so much to my recovery.

Michael D. Hoffman
August 15, 2013

Acknowledgments

With respect to my healing journey and my attempts to live a full, complete, and healthy life despite the abuse I endured, I have found inspiration and support from many people. I was ashamed of what happened to me when I was a boy and afraid of what other people would think of me if they knew. Each person I have told my story of child sexual abuse to, however, has responded with endless acts of kindness, decency, and compassion. For that, I am sincerely grateful.

No longer holding back years of my life from my family and friends, I feel free after writing this little book. Make no mistake, I still struggle with the memories that can trigger pain and sadness and cause disruption in my life, but I hope my story will encourage other childhood abuse survivors to be themselves.

Thank you to the staff of the Office for the Protection of Children and Youth of the Archdiocese of Chicago and to Cardinal Francis George directly for reaching out to me and other survivors of clergy abuse. Your efforts have helped me on my healing journey, and as you continue to reach out to other victim/survivors and their families, I believe you will help heal the wounds caused by clergy abuse and cover-up, especially as it has affected our overall Church.

Thank you to my parish, St. Mary of the Woods in the Edgebrook neighborhood of Chicago, for being such a dynamic and vibrant place to send our kids to school and to worship together. You have helped me heal without even knowing I was hurting, and you have come together to support me and my family since I have come forward with my story.

Thank you to the healing garden planning committee, Holy Family Parish, St. Ignatius College Prep, and all who helped make the healing garden into a beautiful reality. I hope that in its own way, the healing garden helps many other survivors deal with what was done to them through no fault of their own.

Thank you to Fr. Larry Dowling, Fr. Jerry Boland, Fr. Greg Sakowicz, and Fr. Pat Cecil — pastors all, in the best sense of that word. Each of you are blessed with a glorious priestly vocation, and each of you have helped me in so many ways.

Thank you to Fr. Mike McGovern, the current pastor of St. Mary's Parish in Lake Forest. You helped me return to the scene of my abuse and overcome the demons I feared there. My Catholic identity was formed at St. Mary's as a young boy, despite my being sexual abused there by a bad priest. Through my most difficult heartache and despair, the one thing I did not lose is my faith in a loving God, and that is a tribute to the people and staff at St. Mary's.

Thank you to my parents, Darryl and Mary Ellen Hoffman, who remained good Catholics even after they learned they had been betrayed in the most terrible way by a priest. You befriended, trusted, and believed in him. He returned your genuine affection by abusing me, and he manipulated and disrupted our entire family. Through the pain and sadness you have had to deal with since I finally told you what happened to me, you have kept your hope and belief in the goodness of God, which has inspired me to do the same.

Finally, thank you to my wife, Kathy Hoffman. Telling you my story of being sexually abused as a young boy by a priest remains the single most important act of recovery for me. You heard the depth of my sorrow, and you loved me. That's all I ever wanted.

Other Books on Healing and Reconciliation

Taking Back Our Lives:
Reflections for the Survivors of Childhood Abuse
Patti Sherlock
Child-abuse survivor and author Patti Sherlock is a sensitive spiritual
companion for adults who were abused physically, mentally, verbally,
or sexually as children.
144-page paperback, $9.95

The Forgiveness Book: A Catholic Approach
Alice Camille and Fr. Paul Boudreau
Award-winning authors Alice Camille and Paul Boudreau thoroughly
examine what Catholicism has to say about what it takes to
accomplish the difficult act of forgiveness.
112-page paperback, $10.95

Hidden Presence:
12 Blessings That Transformed Sorrow or Loss
Edited by Gregory F. Augustine Pierce
A collection of twelve short stories about bad things that happened in
the lives of the authors, out of which, ultimately, came good things.
176-page hardcover, $9.95

The Geography of God's Mercy:
Stories of Compassion and Forgiveness
Fr. Patrick Hannon, CSC
Award-winning author Patrick Hannon, a Holy Cross priest, offers a
collection of stunning personal stories that delve into the meaning of
reconciliation.
160-page hardcover, $17.95, paperback, $12.95

Available from booksellers nationwide
www.actapublications.com or 800-397-2282